THE 100 BEST
BIBLE VERSES
ON PRAYER

The
100
BEST
BIBLE VERSES
on
PRAYER

TROY SCHMIDT

BETHANYHOUSE

a division of Baker Publishing Group
Minneapolis, Minnesota

Published by Bethany House Publishers
11400 Hampshire Avenue South
Bloomington, Minnesota 55438
www.bethanyhouse.com

Bethany House Publishers is a division of
Baker Publishing Group, Grand Rapids, Michigan

Printed in the United States of America

Library of Congress Cataloging-in-Publication Data is available at the Library of
Congress in Washington, D.C.

ISBN 978-0-7642-1758-6

Scripture quotations, unless otherwise noted, are from the Holy Bible, New Interna-
tional Version®. NIV®. Copyright © 1973, 1978, 1984, 2011 by Biblica, Inc.™ Used
by permission of Zondervan. All rights reserved worldwide. www.zondervan.com

Scripture quotations marked NRSV are from the New Revised Standard Version of
the Bible, copyright © 1989, by the Division of Christian Education of the National
Council of the Churches of Christ in the United States of America. Used by permission. All rights reserved.

Scripture quotations marked NKJV are from the New King James Version. Copyright
© 1982 by Thomas Nelson, Inc. Used by permission. All rights reserved.

Scripture quotations marked NASB are from the New American Standard Bible®, copyright © 1960, 1962, 1963, 1968, 1971, 1972, 1973, 1975, 1977, 1995 by The Lockman
Foundation. Used by permission.

Cover design by Dual Identity

The author is represented by Working Title Agency

16 17 18 19 20 21 22   7 6 5 4 3 2 1

For Barbie,

whose prayers strengthened me when I was weak
and shaped me into the person I am today.

INTRODUCTION

Most people will say they pray.

From the deeply religious to the casual participant, people admit, to some degree, that prayer is an important part of their spiritual activity.

However, ask them in what area of their spiritual life do they need the most help, and most will say prayer.

So most of us are praying, but we're not so good at—or at least not very consistent.

That's probably why in Luke 11:1 we read: "One day Jesus was praying in a certain place. When he finished, one of his disciples said to him, 'Lord, teach us to pray, just as John taught his disciples.'"

Even Jesus' disciples recognized how lacking their prayer life was. They needed help, so they turned to best the pray-er they knew—Jesus.

Prayer is a crazy thing. It's unlike any other conversation we have on earth. When we talk to someone, we generally look into their eyes, make hand gestures, wait for their response, study their body language, listen for voice inflections; in short, it's a two-way thing.

With prayer, you're talking out loud, or in your mind, to an invisible God. You can't see His eyes or facial expressions. No body-language cues. And, most of all, not a sound is heard in response. We have to treat prayer differently to make it more effective.

Prayer is a faith conversation. You talk to God as you would talk to a friend, your father, your brother, or a king, and you trust that He hears you and that He cares about what you have to say. You must know that a response is coming, but it won't be a verbal "I'm on it" from heaven. You have to work hard to see the signs of an answer and sense the Spirit's nudging.

Most of all, we need the assurance of knowing what the Bible says about prayer. Throughout the Old and New Testaments, the Bible repeatedly emphasizes the necessity of prayer and reveals the keys to an effective prayer life.

In this book, I've gleaned the 100 top verses from hundreds of verses about prayer. I selected the ones I felt showed the importance of this spiritual discipline and revealed inspiring reasons to pray. Writing this book has changed my prayer life, and I hope it will bring a new purpose and passion to yours as well.

Troy Schmidt
Windermere, FL
January 2015

GENESIS 24:45

"Before I finished praying in my heart, Rebekah came out, with her jar on her shoulder. She went down to the spring and drew water, and I said to her, 'Please give me a drink.'"

Abraham sent his son Isaac's servant on a mission—"Find a wife for my son!" No simple task in those days. No Jewish Mingle or BC Harmony to go to for help.
All Isaac's servant had to go on was prayer.

The great thing we learn about prayer from this verse is how rapidly God can answer prayer. *Before* the servant finished praying, it says, the answer walked up—Rebekah.

We wish all our prayers were answered that quickly, walking up and announcing their arrival while we're on our knees. It usually doesn't happen that way, but it can.

Pray believing God is answering your prayer right now, and the answer could be coming your way as you speak.

GENESIS 25:21

Isaac prayed to the LORD on behalf of his wife, because she was childless. The LORD answered his prayer, and his wife Rebekah became pregnant.

Being childless is painful for couples who want children. God created us with the desire to be parents, since we have in us the image of God who presents himself as our Father. Couples who are childless wonder why they can't do what God intended for them to do and what their bodies were designed to do—be fruitful and multiply.

Sadly, not everyone who prays for a child gets a child. God's will and plan for our lives is sometimes a mystery.

So what is God's will, and how do we pray for it?

Through stories like that of Isaac and Rebekah (and many others in the Bible), we know God desires to make those who are barren fertile. He wants us to be fruitful, challenging us to be more patient, more trusting, more compassionate, through whatever challenges we face.

Through this story, we see that God wants husbands to love their wives during trying times. Despite their frustration at not being able to have children, Isaac loved his wife and prayed for her. Their love was alive and well, no matter what setbacks they faced. That kind of selfless love God uses to do amazing things.

Prayer lays the groundwork for God to step in and bless us. He can bring life to those unresponsive areas of our lives in ways we never imagined.

EXODUS 8:28

So Pharaoh said, "I will let you go to sacrifice to the LORD your God in the wilderness, provided you do not go very far away. Pray for me." (NRSV)

The plagues ripped through Egypt, destroying its economy and infrastructure. Pharaoh, the boss, teetered back and forth between permitting the Israelites to go and forcing them back into slavery. The battle tore up Pharaoh's heart.

Here Moses' enemy asked for prayer, even though Pharaoh's actions showed he didn't believe in prayer or the one to whom Moses would pray.

Moses did pray for the situation, but Pharaoh hardened his heart and changed his mind, taking back his offer and forcing the Israelites to remain as slaves.

Sometimes we have to pray for people for whom it doesn't seem to do any good. These friends, family members, or leaders seem close to surrendering to God, only to turn away at the last minute.

That's OK. Keep on praying for them. You don't always know or see what God is doing.

Secretly, most people want to be prayed for, no matter how defensive they are about God. They need to know that their names are being presented to the Almighty. They need to see God clearly answering those prayers.

How they respond is between them and God. All you can do is pray.

NUMBERS 21:7

Therefore the people came to Moses, and said, "We have sinned, for we have spoken against the LORD and against you; pray to the LORD that He take away the serpents from us." So Moses prayed for the people. (NKJV)

The snake infestation came upon the Israelites because of their grumbling and disobedience. It was their fault and they deserved it. However, when they turned to Moses for prayer, Moses didn't say, "Hey, you dug your own graves! Save yourselves!" Instead, he prayed for them.

It's hard to pray for people who deserve the mess they are in. Sure, we want them to learn their lesson and grow in their relationship with God, but to leave them alone in their suffering is unkind.

We must show grace and mercy because God has shown grace and mercy to us. Maybe we didn't commit adultery or blow up a building like someone else, but we've had lustful thoughts, covetous thoughts, or hateful thoughts. Sin is sin.

God wants us to pray for all people who are suffering. One day we may face a similar hardship. Then we will want people to pray for us as we suffer the consequences of our actions and find restoration.

DEUTERONOMY 4:7

"What other nation is so great as to have their gods near them the way the LORD our God is near us whenever we pray to him?"

God created Israel as a nation unlike any other nation. It would be a nation that sacrificed their treasures to their God, that treated all people fairly and justly, from the top down, and that enforced order and morality through their laws. God powerfully displayed His favor through miracles in Israel that were talked about in other nations.

Moses points out in this verse that prayer kept God close to the nation of Israel. It was something no other nation could boast because they worshiped false gods. Israel had a relationship with the one true God. And it set them apart.

We want our nation to be that great nation. A nation that follows the one true God. A righteous nation that gives generously to others and treats all people fairly and justly—a nation where God can work and reveal himself powerfully.

We need to ask God to bless and preserve our country. A nation can only be great when their God is the one true God of Abraham, Isaac, and Jacob.

JUDGES 16:28

Then Samson prayed to the LORD, "Sovereign LORD, remember me. Please, God, strengthen me just once more,
and let me with one blow get revenge on the Philistines
for my two eyes."

Samson started out great. His birth was prophesied by
an angel. His parents were excited about the arrival of
their son. If he had only followed a few simple rules, his
strength would have been unstoppable, and God could have
used him more powerfully.

However, Samson grew up to be a disappointment to others. He didn't follow the rules, and he used his own strength to
get whatever he wanted—not what God wanted (God did use
Samson's arrogance for His purposes). Samson got caught in his
own trap, captured by his enemies, and mocked by thousands.

In his final moments, Samson prayed to be used mightily
one last time. Even though his life did not shape up to what
was hoped, Samson felt he could do more. So he prayed for one
last sacrificial opportunity to be used by God. God answered
that prayer.

No matter where we are in our lives or what crises we face,
we can pray that God will not give up on us, despite our failures,
and that He use us one more time in a powerful way.

1 SAMUEL 1:10

She, greatly distressed, prayed to the LORD and wept bitterly. (NASB)

What does an anguished, distressed prayer look like? It could include a lot of uncontrollable weeping for starters. The tears could be so heavy and the body so agonized, that to an outsider it might appear the person is drunk. At least that's what Eli the priest thought when he saw Hannah praying.

This kind of prayer comes from deep within one's soul—not just words from their lips. The person has reached the end of their resources. Their prayer expresses the pain of loss and passionately cries out to God for help. The prayer is desperate.

God responds to our sincere cries for help. He responded to the cry of the Israelites suffering in Egypt. Jesus healed the afflicted when they pleaded for His mercy and grace.

If your prayers aren't anguished, maybe they aren't sincere. Maybe you don't really trust God to hear you and answer. Maybe you feel "things will just work out" or "prayers don't really make any difference." Maybe you don't really care.

Over and over in the Bible, we see that when people prayed passionately, God responded. Their cares became God's cares. So pray deeply, from the heart, believing God hears you and answers. And don't worry about what other people think.

1 SAMUEL 1:27

"For this child I prayed, and the LORD has granted me my petition which I asked of Him." (NKJV)

H annah was barren. She prayed for a child, and God heard her prayer and answered, giving her the child she requested (and whom she had dedicated to serve in the temple).

We continue to pray for children God gives us as they grow up. When they are young, we tell them what to do and they do it (mostly).

But when they grow up, it's a different story. They have free will and decide their own fate. It's hard for a parent to watch a child make poor decisions that result in severe consequences or even a poorly chosen path in life.

Apart from giving advice, a parent can only pray for a child, asking God to intervene. It's a wonderful thing when God does what we have asked of Him. The Lord's will is supreme, and He sees our lives from His perspective. For Him to hear our prayer and answer it is a blessing.

So pray for those children who won't listen to you, and thank God for those who do. May He grant what you ask for, according to His will.

1 SAMUEL 12:23

"As for me, far be it from me that I should sin against the LORD by failing to pray for you. And I will teach you the way that is good and right."

I s it a sin not to pray?

Samuel the prophet thought so. As he spoke to the people and confronted them about their sin, he encouraged them not to turn to idols and to serve only God faithfully. His role, as a teacher and guide, necessitated his connection to God spiritually, done entirely by prayer.

So for a prophet, prayer is at the top of his job description. If he didn't connect with God, he would be leading the people according to his own free will. Always dangerous.

Just before Samuel spoke these words, he called on God, and He responded to his request with thunder and rain. The people were impressed and knew Samuel was a man of God.

Leading people without prayer would be a sin. You can't teach people what is good and right, and you won't see the power of God to back you up if you don't ask for it.

Without prayer, it would just be all about you.

2 SAMUEL 7:18

Then King David went in and sat before the LORD, and he said: "Who am I, Sovereign LORD, and what is my family, that you have brought me this far?"

Our prayer time should begin with these thoughts: *Who am I? Why me? Why would you listen to my prayers? Why would you bless me and my family?*

Of all people, it would seem unlikely that David would begin his prayer time in this way. King David was *the* man! He killed the giant that mocked Israel. He established Israel as a nation. He defeated thousands of their enemies. He wrote chart-topping psalms. He developed plans to build the temple.

But even David prayed, amazed that God would use him—a simple shepherd boy—and bring him this far. David never forgot his roots. He still remembered his days watching the flocks, forgotten by his brothers. The lunch delivery boy later called up to deliver Goliath's head.

No matter who you are or what you've done, pray humbly. You can't become a person after God's own heart, like David, without first humbling yourself.

2 SAMUEL 7:27

"For you, O LORD of hosts, the God of Israel, have made this revelation to your servant, saying, 'I will build you a house'; therefore your servant has found courage to pray this prayer to you." (NRSV)

Imagine if you needed courage to pray.

"Okay, God, I can't believe I'm going to say this, but here goes . . ."

King David had the courage to pray about the building of the temple because he sensed God's leading him to build it. This was the ultimate building project of his day, the greatest architectural wonder of the time.

As we pray, we should be willing to go out on a limb, having the courage to say the hard things. Knowing God's leading in a matter gives us the courage to ask. The outcome could shake up our lives. But our confidence is in God.

David's commitment to prayer was expensive and took a lot of his time. You could say it created jobs, but it also created headaches. The prayer established his legacy as a godly man and set the bar high in his life.

Prayer time should not be all about seeking our own comfort. It should be about seeking God's will, and that alone could make things somewhat uncomfortable for you.

Are you bold enough to pray that kind of prayer?

2 SAMUEL 24:25

And David built there an altar to the LORD, and offered burnt offerings and peace offerings. So the LORD heeded the prayers for the land, and the plague was withdrawn from Israel. (NKJV)

David made a huge mistake. He had his people counted to determine his nation's strength. Basically, he was putting his trust in numbers more than in God. Taking a census is not a sin. Trusting in those numbers more than God is.

So God sent a plague to Israel that killed thousands of people. God responded to David's number-conscious faith by removing numbers of people from his country (like 70,000).

David realized his mistake, repented, and prayed for God to stop the slaughter.

We've made some serious mistakes too. Maybe 70,000 people haven't died, but our lack of faith in God and trust in other things like money, work, or pleasure affect other people in the process. In the end, the numbers add up.

We should be asking God to show us our mistakes and our priorities, and reveal to us how we are hurting others through our choices. The numbers could devastate us.

1 KINGS 8:30

"Hear the supplication of your servant and of your people Israel when they pray toward this place. Hear from heaven, your dwelling place, and when you hear, forgive."

Solomon prayed at the temple dedication ceremony, asking God to use this location to promote prayer. When the Israelites prayed, they turned toward the temple, the earthly representative of God's home.

Solomon asked God to hear their prayers from heaven, and not only to hear, but to forgive. Of all the things we ask God to do in prayer, forgiving our sins tops the list.

If God healed your cancer or gave you that job you were seeking, great, but if your sins are not forgiven, what good will health and wealth do?

When Jesus healed the paralytic who was lowered in from the roof by his friends, He first forgave him his sins. Better to go through life physically paralyzed than eternally lost.

As we pray from our homes, we are focused toward God in our heavenly home. Forgiveness opens the door to that eternal place.

1 KINGS 13:6

> Then the king said to the man of God, "Intercede with the LORD your God and pray for me that my hand may be restored." So the man of God interceded with the LORD, and the king's hand was restored and became as it was before.

Praying for restoration is probably the number-one intercessory prayer we can offer.

King Jeroboam was far from God, worshiping at a temple not approved by God. He wanted to start his own branch of Judaism. A man of God emerged and cursed the unsanctioned temple, and when Jeroboam reached out his hand to point at the intruder, his hand shriveled up. Now Jeroboam turned to the man for help, asking that his hand be restored.

The king wanted his hand to be made whole, but his real need was restoration of his soul. When Jeroboam followed his own inclination, he encouraged a relationship with himself instead of a relationship with God. His sin separated him from God.

Interceding for physical restoration is always in order, but relational restoration with God is of greater importance. A physical problem could be the key to turning someone back to God.

1 KINGS 19:4

He . . . went a day's journey into the wilderness. He came to a broom bush, sat down under it and prayed that he might die. "I have had enough, LORD," he said. "Take my life; I am no better than my ancestors."

Elijah was having a bad day. After a great victory on Mount Carmel, he found himself on the queen's most-wanted list. He thought he had eradicated all his enemies, until he found them getting stronger and more vehement.

Elijah became overwhelmed and depressed. He asked God to take him.

Praying when depressed is the best remedy. It confirms our utter weakness, and through prayer we surrender ourselves to God. We realize there's nothing more we can do on our own.

Maybe that's just where God wants us. To ask for death—the complete extinction of self, that is. Not physical death, as a way of escape, but death to self, death to our own way and our own resources. To many, death to self feels like uselessness or senselessness.

To God, it looks like the perfect place to start.

So if you are at the end of your rope, pray, and let God show you the path to His will for your life.

2 KINGS 6:17

Then Elisha prayed and said, "O LORD, I pray, open his eyes that he may see." And the LORD opened the servant's eyes and he saw; and behold, the mountain was full of horses and chariots of fire all around Elisha. (NASB)

Elisha's servant thought they were doomed. The city was surrounded by chariots and horses. The enemy army had them trapped.

But Elisha didn't panic. He knew there was another army out there, one unseen by the human eye, and many times more powerful.

So he prayed that the servant's eyes would be opened, and the man saw the invisible army of the Lord. The enemy was outnumbered, and they didn't even know it.

When we or those we love feel overwhelmed and trapped by the enemy, it's time to pray for reinforcements. The army of the Lord is encamped around His people; through prayer and by faith we can know the power of His protection to thwart the armies of darkness. Our victory is in the name of the Lord.

We may not be able to physically see it, but we can pray that we will know it, and be strengthened and encouraged that we are not alone.

1 CHRONICLES 5:20

They were helped against them, and the Hagrites and all
who were with them were given into their hand; for they
cried out to God in the battle, and He answered their
prayers because they trusted in Him. (NASB)

Who do you trust in wartime? Psalm 20 says some trust
in chariots and some in horses. It's to the weaponry
and the backup that most people look for security.
The more chariots . . . the more horses . . . the more victories . . .
right?

This verse is talking about the Reubenites, the Gadites, and
the half-tribe of Manasseh, and their war against the Hagrites,
Jetur, Naphish, and Nodab. The tribes of Israel had plenty
of men, yet still they cried out to God. They didn't tell God,
"Thanks, we've got this." They cried out to God in the battle,
and He answered their prayers.

Whatever trial or battle you may be facing, pray, trusting that
you are not alone. You may have lawyers on your side, friends'
support, or experience in this kind of thing, but trust God to
bring you the victory. He has resources and weapons to bring
to the battle that you didn't know were available.

2 CHRONICLES 7:14

"If my people, who are called by my name, will humble themselves and pray and seek my face and turn from their wicked ways, then I will hear from heaven, and I will forgive their sin and will heal their land."

People want their nation to be more godly. They want the God-honoring beginnings of their nation to be restored. They want laws that reflect Christian values and leaders who are true Christ followers.

How can we see that happen? We must begin by humbling ourselves, not asking God to humble our leaders. Humbling always begins with the people of God. It's the Christians who must turn from their wicked ways. No one can point their fingers at someone else. Revival begins in the house of God, not in the House of Representatives.

It is after we humble ourselves, pray, seek God, and turn from our own wickedness that God will hear our prayers, forgive our sins, and heal our land.

Prayer can change a nation after God's people, the ones who are called by His name, set the example and live as God has called them to live.

2 CHRONICLES 30:27

The priests and the Levites stood to bless the people, and God heard them, for their prayer reached heaven, his holy dwelling place.

Church leaders, when you pray for your people, God hears you. Your prayers reach heaven.

The priests and the Levites were the first religious leaders in the Bible whose full-time job was to focus on the spiritual welfare of the people. Their own prayer life with God enabled them to guide the people aright.

At times they stood to offer a blessing on the people, a benediction of sorts that redirected their connection with God by saying the words God would say to His people.

In Old Testament times, the priests acted as the conduit to God. Today, because of Jesus Christ, we have direct access to God the Father through His Son, though the prayers and blessings of spiritual leaders are still important to us and serve as God's voice of comfort and direction to His people.

2 CHRONICLES 32:24

In those days Hezekiah became sick and was at the point of death. He prayed to the LORD, and he answered him and gave him a sign. (NRSV)

Hezekiah was at death's door.

The king prayed for healing and God answered him, adding fifteen years to his life (Isaiah 38:5). A true miracle.

This kind of prayer for the dying has been prayed by millions since then with varying results. Why was Hezekiah favored? Did his kingly status warrant special treatment?

Hezekiah survived to show that God has power over death. The incident was meant to show the power of prayer, not to show a precedent for all similar prayers. God's mercy is shown in different ways in different circumstances.

Actually, Hezekiah's extra fifteen years were not lived well. During his "bonus years," he showed off his treasuries to envoys from Babylon who eventually looted Jerusalem and burned it to the ground. Hezekiah prayed for a longer life but didn't live it wisely.

Later in the chapter, it says, "God left him to himself, in order to test him and to know all that was in his heart" (v. 31).

If you pray for more years, will you live them well? Maybe God ends a life to save it from more catastrophe and bad choices.

EZRA 9:6

"I am too ashamed and disgraced, my God, to lift up my face to you, because our sins are higher than our heads and our guilt has reached to the heavens."

Ezra wanted to see the restoration of Israel after the invasions of the Assyrians and Babylonians. Now with the Persians in power, Israel had a chance to be the great nation it once was.

But Ezra saw the pattern of his people who returned once again to the sins that got them into trouble in the first place. So he prayed, full of shame. Not his shame. He was ashamed of his people. These sins were offensive to God and were happening right before Ezra's eyes!

We can be disappointed in our community, our church, or our country, and pray a corporate prayer that God would accept our plea and forgive others, pleading that God not judge all of us because of them.

We may not be part of the problem, but we can be part of the solution.

EZRA 10:1

While Ezra prayed and made confession, weeping and throwing himself down before the house of God, a very great assembly of men, women, and children gathered to him out of Israel; the people also wept bitterly. (NRSV)

Ezra's prayers became physical workouts—weeping loudly and throwing himself down before God.

Should prayers always be quiet and peaceful, with the simple bowing of your head and the gentle folding of your hands? It depends on what you are praying for and how passionate you are about your prayer. Sometimes it depends on how much you care.

While this prayer seems over-the-top, Ezra was praying that God not judge the reformed nation because the people returned to their old sins. It was desperate and urgent.

Ezra wasn't afraid to pray this way in public, and yet it wasn't showy, like the kind of public prayers for which Jesus reprimanded the Pharisees. Ezra prayed genuinely, from the heart. This was not a display for attention but a demand for action—to motivate the people to stop sinning and to ask God to start forgiving.

Be passionate when you pray, but be genuine too. Sometimes it may turn into a workout.

NEHEMIAH 1:4

So it was, when I heard these words, that I sat down and wept, and mourned for many days; I was fasting and praying before the God of heaven. (NKJV)

What was it that caused Nehemiah so much pain and anguish that he mourned, fasted, and prayed before God?

A wall.

That's right, a simple wall. Well, that wall surrounded a very special city—Jerusalem—once a great city, now a dilapidated ruin. The disrepair of the wall meant Jerusalem was vulnerable to attack from its enemies.

So Nehemiah prayed for the city. Did he pray for the wall to be miraculously built up overnight by invisible angels? No. He prayed that somebody would have the resources and influence to rebuild the wall. Who would that be?

It would be Nehemiah himself.

Nehemiah's position as the cupbearer gave him special access to the king, who granted him permission and the resources to rebuild the wall. Nehemiah prayed and he became the answer.

Our passion can turn to action when we pray, but the answer to our prayer may be ourselves.

NEHEMIAH 4:9

So we prayed to our God, and set a guard as a protection against them day and night. (NRSV)

S hould I pray, or should I act? That is the question.

If I truly have faith in God, should I be out there making things happen and accomplishing the tasks associated with my prayer, or should I just sit back and let God make it happen?

Both.

Nehemiah faced opposition rebuilding the wall, so he prayed for the protection of the city and the safety of the workers. They posted guards around the clock. Even the builders swung a hammer with one hand and carried a sword in the other. Was this demonstrating a lack of faith?

No. This was accepting the reality of the situation. These men were in a dangerous place. They needed to protect themselves. Besides, God could have used the guards to give the workers confidence to carry on and also put fear in the enemy around them. The presence of the guards could have been part of the answer to their prayers.

Praying with faith doesn't mean praying without common sense or without using all the resources at our disposal.

JOB 42:8

"My servant Job will pray for you, and I will accept his prayer and not deal with you according to your folly. You have not spoken the truth about me, as my servant Job has."

God wrapped up the book of Job by telling Job's friends—Eliphaz, Bildad, and Zophar—whose advice angered God, that Job would pray for them and that his prayer would protect them from God's wrath.

Imagine that: a person's prayer can protect someone from God's wrath.

You can be a bodyguard for a loved one who doesn't know how damaging their actions are to others. Prayer is the ultimate secret service tactic, as you intercede for someone's safety completely undetected. Prayer is enlisting in the C.I.A.—Calling In Angels—for spiritual reinforcements.

Prayer time takes on a new meaning when you see yourself as the prayer police, always on call to serve and to protect.

PSALM 5:2

Listen to the sound of my cry, my King and my God, for
to you I pray. (NRSV)

H elp! I need a King and a God!"
  Both titles speak of authority. When one cries for
a higher authority, he sees the limitations of his own
power. Someone who doesn't cry out for help thinks he can
handle things himself. He is greatly mistaken and can make
the situation even worse.

The titles King and God cover the earthly and the heavenly
realms. King is a title for earthly authority (applicable also to
God, of course, as is the case in this prayer), and God is a title
exclusively for heavenly authority (though some on earth think
they are gods). By crying out to both, you are covering both
territories, the seen and unseen, here and there.

Don't cry out to a servant or an assistant or a receptionist.
Desperation calls for your King and your God. Let Him take
charge and take care of your situation.

Go right to the boss.

PSALM 35:13

Yet when they were ill, I put on sackcloth and humbled myself with fasting. When my prayers returned to me unanswered, I went about mourning as though for my friend or brother.

Despite the desperate plea for a sick person, the psalmist—who even puts on sackcloth and fasts—felt his prayer went unanswered. Is that true?

Our prayers are not like the text messages that we ignore. We know our response to that person's request will set off a chain of lengthy replies or create more work for us, so we pretend we didn't receive the text in the first place.

God gets our prayer request and He does respond. While our need may seem to be ignored, the answer could be "not yet" or "no." Both of these are answers, though they may not be the answers we were looking for. Maybe the timing is not right, or God is working on our faith, or someone else's, by delaying His response. (Remember, God sees the bigger picture.)

Either way, we cannot say that God ignores our prayers. He always answers, but not always in the way or time we prefer.

PSALM 55:1

Listen to my prayer, O God, do not ignore my plea.

Ignoring someone is the greatest show of disrespect. Teachers hate it. Parents despise it. Cops don't tolerate it. Ignoring someone says, "Your intentions make no difference to me, and I choose not to consider them."

This cannot be God's response to our prayers. His love for us requires His attention to our prayers. He cannot ignore us.

We plead with God not to ignore us, and yet we frequently ignore Him. We choose not to listen to His voice in our hearts that calls us to serve, or to stand up for Him, or to say no to temptation. We are comfortable with hitting God's mute button because He inhibits our way of life.

God knows perfectly well what it's like to be ignored, yet He would never ignore His children. His love turns up the volume on our prayer requests. He wants to hear us; in fact, He can't wait to hear from us.

If we know how it feels to be ignored, why do we ignore God?

29

PSALM 66:20

Blessed be God, who has not turned away my prayer, nor
His mercy from me! (NKJV)

Rejection hurts. A rejection letter says you're not the
right person. The stamp of rejection hits the very core
of our self-esteem, telling us we're not good enough or
worthy of one's time or resources.

Talk to any "Dear John" about the damage done by rejection. Even those commonly heard phrases like "We're going in
different directions" or "Maybe we can just be friends" or "It's
me, not you" don't fool anyone. It's still rejection.

No matter who it comes from, rejection feels like the cold,
hard stamp of disapproval, slammed down on our request by
a disgruntled office worker who hates his job and doesn't care
about our feelings or situation in life. "Rejected! Next!"

God does not reject a sincere prayer request. Every request
that crosses His desk is carefully considered and lovingly answered. There are no cold, hard stamps of disapproval. No
trash cans or shredders around to toss our prayer. Even His
in-box isn't backed up.

Your prayer request is being processed. Guaranteed.

PSALM 69:13

But I pray to you, LORD, in the time of your favor; in your great love, O God, answer me with your sure salvation.

T he answer to every prayer is salvation. It's the only answer we need.

We want life, and we cry out for help to be saved from death and destruction. God wants to give us salvation, and every prayer request is answered with salvation in mind.

While God can and does save us from financial ruin, relationship failures, and health issues—giving us new life while we're on the earth—He ultimately offers us salvation, restoration, and redemption, even when His answer might be "no" to our specific request. Our business could collapse, our marriage could end, and cancer could consume us, but the final answer to those prayers is always salvation for those who believe.

And don't miss the comfort of that powerful word *sure* before *salvation*. Our salvation is assured. Not hoped for or wished for. It is certain.

What answer could be better?

PSALM 86:1

Hear me, LORD, and answer me, for I am poor and needy.

O ur prayers should recognize our current state—poor and needy.

And let's be honest. If we're praying, we must be poor and needy.

Why would we want God to hear us and answer our prayer unless we needed something from Him?

We may have money in our checking account and plenty of food in our pantry, but there could be a deficit in our career path, a waning in our passion for life. We could be overdrawn in our relationships or running dry in patience, compassion, and focus.

There will never be a time when we have nothing to pray about. Life on this earth drains and challenges us, leaving us all poor and needy. Even if we don't feel that way now, we will at some point.

As long as we exist on this earth, we will be poor and needy. Not until we enter our eternal home in heaven will we be rich and have need of nothing.

Until then, keep praying.

PSALM 141:2

May my prayer be set before you like incense; may the lifting up of my hands be like the evening sacrifice.

Incense and sacrifice were part of the Old Testament worship ritual.

The incense stood for prayer, as it symbolically rose to the heavens, leaving a pleasant scent as it filled the room.

The sacrifice stood for confession and forgiveness, as sins were remembered and an animal was killed as a sacrifice to appease God's wrath.

The Old Testament rituals are gone, but their essence remains.

We pray, lifting up our hearts and hands to worship God, and our words rise as a sweet-smelling sacrifice.

We pray, confessing our sins and receiving forgiveness. Christ became our substitute on the cross, the ultimate sacrifice, so that no animal sacrifice is necessary. We give ourselves to God, holy and pleasing in His sight.

We don't have to go to the temple to pray. Our bodies are the temples of the Holy Spirit and our hearts act as the altar.

PSALM 143:1

LORD, hear my prayer, listen to my cry for mercy; in your
faithfulness and righteousness come to my relief.

Prayer connects the cry to the relief, the problem to the
solution.

The cry calls for God's mercy. His faithfulness and
righteousness come to our rescue. God's desire for His children
assures His faithfulness to us.

His Fatherly love always comes running.

His righteousness assures the right and best answer. We can
trust God's judgment in any situation. He knows what is best
for all concerned.

So cry out to the Lord and know that relief is coming. Our
faithful and righteous God is on His way.

PROVERBS 15:8

The LORD detests the sacrifice of the wicked, but the prayer of the upright pleases him.

Sacrifice or prayer. Which does God prefer?

Both require some effort. Either forces you to give up something. Both, when done properly, exalt God and call Him worthy. What concerns God is our motivation for both.

The person who parades into the church and makes sure everyone sees him putting his offering in the basket is doing it for show. This kind of sacrifice is detestable to God.

Personal prayer, done properly, is done in private and does not draw the attention of others. Public prayer is done humbly, beseeching God for others, not drawing attention because of our spiritual vocabulary or articulate passion.

The sacrifice of the wicked or ungrateful has no value in God's eyes.

But when those who live uprightly pray and give, God smiles. They are not seeking the praise of others, but only the honor and glory of God.

PROVERBS 28:9

If anyone turns a deaf ear to my instruction, even their prayers are detestable.

People who love to talk about themselves don't tend to take advice very well. It's more important for them to be heard than to make any changes. They don't want to hear how to improve their lives. They are more interested in making an impression.

That kind of attitude doesn't work very well with prayer, either. We have to have a heart that listens as well as speaks, with more emphasis on hearing from God than on talking to God.

This verse tells us that someone who rejects God's instruction, or is too busy to listen to God, churns out prayers that are detestable to God.

The Hebrew word *tow'ebah* translates to mean "reprehensible, disgusting, an abomination." The prayers of the disobedient are an abomination to God. That's a pretty serious reaction.

So our obedience leads to God's hearing our prayers. Don't turn a deaf ear to God. Listen and obey, and your prayers will speak volumes.

ISAIAH 1:15

When you spread out your hands, I will hide My eyes from
you; Even though you make many prayers, I will not hear.
Your hands are full of blood. (NKJV)

Many people pray with their hands folded as a sign of
submission and pleading. Others open their hands to
show their willingness to receive God's instruction and
blessing. Some may pray with their hands raised heavenward
to communicate the surrender of their hearts.

The context of this verse is the initial call of Isaiah as a
prophet. The nation of Israel had split, and the northern nations,
ten of the original tribes, sinned greatly, and God judged them
by allowing the Assyrian nation to wipe them out, scattering
them. The southern nation, called Judah, hung in there with two
tribes; however, they were succumbing to the same sins as their
northern brothers. Isaiah's prophecies pointed out their problems and pointed to a solution—repentance and obedience. The
southern nation refused and eventually fell to the Babylonians.

Isaiah said the people's hands were spread out to receive God's
blessing; however, their hearts were not prepared to receive God's
instruction. They were disobedient and self-centered, and God
saw their hands as full of blood. Whose blood was on their
hands? The blood of innocent people they hurt or ignored. Those
whom God told them to love and they chose to hate.

So look at your hands before you pray. Are they clean? If
not, cleanse them through confession and repentance and then
follow God's leading as to what you should do next.

ISAIAH 38:2

Then Hezekiah turned his face toward the wall, and prayed
to the Lord. (NKJV)

There are times in our lives when we feel like we're talking to a wall.

Our prayers seem as effective as asking a pile of stones to help us with our greatest need. We feel like we're hitting a wall, a dead end; we're unable to move forward in our lives.

King Hezekiah hit that wall as news about his health came to him. It was not good. He had only days to live.

But instead of being defeated by that wall, Hezekiah prayed toward it, as though his prayers were a battering ram to smash through it. And it worked! God heard his prayer and gave Hezekiah fifteen more years.

We may hear only silence when we pray, and God may seem as communicative as a stone wall, but that's not the case. The only walls we face are obstacles that God can easily break through.

So don't pray *to* that wall . . . pray *through* it . . . and watch it come tumbling down.

ISAIAH 44:17

The rest of it he makes into a god, his idol, bows down to it and worships it; he prays to it and says, "Save me, for you are my god!" (NRSV)

Probably the most reprehensible thing a person could do in Old Testament times was pray to an idol. Over and over God reprimanded His people for adopting the gods of other nations and worshiping them. That kind of heinous act started with the golden calf and continued all the way down to gods with names like Baal, Ashtoreth, and Molech.

By New Testament times, the Jews didn't worship those gods, but instead worshiped tradition and the law, as seen in the power and influence of the Pharisees and Sadducees. As their Old Testament forefathers trusted their idols, the New Testament Jews trusted the law to save them.

We may not have a tangible idol figure in our home, but there may be something common we turn to—to save us from boredom, from reality, from pain, or responsibility. It could be a recreational vehicle, a video game, the Internet, a pill, a bottle, or even food.

Ridiculous, isn't it, to think that someone could be so devoted to or dependent on something in their driveway, on their phone, or in their refrigerator. But in our own unassuming way, we may connect with something (or someone) to which we give more devotion and trust than we give to God.

ISAIAH 64:9

Do not be angry beyond measure, LORD; do not remember our sins forever. Oh, look on us, we pray, for we are all your people.

When was the last time you prayed for God not to be angry with you?

We pray for forgiveness, but often forget God's anger associated with sin. God despises sin because sin separates us from Him.

When we pray for forgiveness, we are asking God not to be angry. Because of Jesus' death on the cross for us, God's wrath is turned away from us, and He sees us as righteous before Him. Remember the feeling you had as a child when your earthly father was so angry with you that he turned his back on you? What a horrible feeling that was!

God is not pleased with our sin, but if we go to Him, asking His forgiveness and pleading the blood of Jesus, His Son, His anger is turned away. We are His people, the sheep of His pasture. Be thankful you have an advocate in Jesus.

Be thankful God's wrath is no longer turned toward you.

JEREMIAH 7:16

"So do not pray for this people nor offer any plea or petition for them; do not plead with me, for I will not listen to you."

Don't pray? How could God tell us not to pray for certain people?

During this extreme circumstance, the people of Jerusalem regularly turned away from God to the point of exile. God vowed to send them to Babylon after the plunder and destruction of Jerusalem. For over three hundred years the people of Judah moved further and further away from God to the point of no return. There was nothing anyone could do. Any repentance by them was just for show and would only be forgotten when they began a new pattern of rebellion.

So God told Jeremiah to tell the people that any prayers or pleading for mercy would be ignored. God had heard it all before.

We never know if those we pray for have crossed the point of no return. It is always best to pray for them anyway. In this case, Jeremiah heard directly from God not to pray for someone.

Unless we've heard otherwise from the Source, we should pray for everyone that they don't reach the point of no return as the people in Jeremiah's day did.

JEREMIAH 29:7

"Also, seek the peace and prosperity of the city to which I have carried you into exile. Pray to the LORD for it, because if it prospers, you too will prosper."

Pray for your city.

Every city has its unique challenges, from its economy to its ecology, from its people to its place on the map, from its weather to its workers.

When we pray for our city, we pray for its prosperity. Yes, that could mean financial blessing in the form of opportunities and jobs. It could mean debt reduction and dream investments, progressing forward with hope. We want to be proud of our city and feel secure there.

But we should also pray for the peace of a city. We may not be at war, but there are tensions that divide people—both racial and economical. Politics can get selfish, focused more on a party than on the people. Unity is prosperity.

We should pray for spiritual revival, that the churches thrive and reach the hearts of people for Christ. Faith brings love and purpose. We want the people of our city to serve one another, not just themselves. Then the city will be truly prosperous.

It's OK to pray for your city's prosperity, but don't focus only on the economical side of things. Pray that God works through the hearts and lives of His people there.

JEREMIAH 42:3

"Pray that the LORD your God will tell us where we should go and what we should do."

We should pray for guidance as to where to go and what to do.

Our mornings should start by receiving our schedule. We prepare our hearts for whatever God has in store, making ourselves available to Him.

Our evenings should end as we debrief our day, asking ourselves and God if everything went as planned and what we can do for a better tomorrow.

Imagine if every morning we received a printout of everything God wanted us to do and every place He wanted us to be. All we had to do was follow every step and show up when asked.

Sound easy? Actually it would not be. To do all God asks us to do and to go wherever He asks us to go means putting ourselves aside. No more "me" time. No more doing it "my way." Our schedule would be void of a lot of shopping, TV watching, playing, and pampering—a lot of things that don't matter for eternity, only for the here and now. While we may feel good at the end of the day, the God-focused schedule might come as a shock to us.

God seeks people who will ask for a God-directed itinerary, those who are willing to do God's will and go where He leads.

43

LAMENTATIONS 3:44

You have covered Yourself with a cloud so that no prayer can pass through. (NASB)

Does God ever cover himself with a sort of prayer cloud so that nothing can get through to Him?

For the writer of Lamentations (most likely Jeremiah) that certainly seemed to be the case. The collapse of Jerusalem and the Jewish faith felt hopeless at the time, as if prayers were not getting through to God. For the Jews, this was their 9/11, and they wondered, "Where is God?" He was there all along, and even warned them that this would happen. But no one had listened.

Obviously God can't *not* hear our prayers, but after years and years of disobedience by His people, God's mind was made up, and no words from anyone would change His mind.

Hopefully we aren't in a situation where God's mind is made up, and He is angry at a nation or a people for decades of dissension and desertion. In our day, that feeling of a prayer ceiling usually comes when we get impatient and want answers *now,* not trusting God to work in His way and in His time.

God hears your prayer, even when you feel the clouds have become a concrete barrier, deflecting your request. Prayers do get through. We just need to wait patiently.

DANIEL 6:7

All the commissioners of the kingdom, the prefects and the satraps, the high officials and the governors have consulted together that the king should establish a statute and enforce an injunction that anyone who makes a petition to any god or man besides you, O king, for thirty days, shall be cast into the lions' den. (NASB)

How important is your prayer time to you? Would you still do it if it were against the law? Would you pray, like Daniel did, with the windows wide open for all the law-enforcement people to see and hear as you prayed out loud? And would you repeat that rebellious action three times a day just in case anyone missed it?

Daniel defied a king's edict not to pray to anyone except the king himself, or that person would have a dinner date with a den of hungry lions.

Are there places in your world where prayer is illegal or at least frowned upon? Could you get into deep trouble if you prayed out loud? Some of us struggle to pray silently in our own living room before everyone wakes up. That would be paradise for Daniel.

Are you afraid to pray in a restaurant before you eat, worried what others will think? How about praying at school, around the flagpole, before classes begin? What about opening a business meeting with prayer? The decision to pray in public in any of these situations should influence the way we conduct ourselves afterward and how people see us.

Maybe that's what we're most afraid of.

DANIEL 9:3

Then I turned to the Lord God, to seek an answer by prayer and supplication with fasting and sackcloth and ashes. (NRSV)

Fasting, sackcloth, and ashes?

Is this what prayer requires?

Hard enough to focus our busy minds away from this world and concentrate on talking to an invisible God, but to make it unpleasant with fasting, sackcloth, and ashes doesn't help.

Actually it does . . .

All three of these unpleasantries reminded people like Daniel to pray. Every rumble of the stomach acted as an alarm clock to tell Daniel to hunger for God. Every itch and scratch of the sackcloth on his skin told Daniel to pray for the discomfort many were feeling. The ashes polluted his hair and soiled his skin, bringing to mind the death we all will one day face, turning to ashes in this fallen, sinful, yet temporary world.

If you have a hard time praying, try fasting, sackcloth, and ashes to remind you to pray. These devices aren't used to impress God with your humility. Use them to keep you more focused when you pray.

DANIEL 9:20

> While I was speaking, and was praying and confessing
> my sin and the sin of my people Israel, and presenting
> my supplication before the LORD my God on behalf of
> the holy mountain of my God—(NRSV)

When you point a finger at someone, there are three more pointed back at you. Cliché, huh? But actually it's true.

Finger-pointing has become somewhat of a sin in our society. We push away a finger pointed in our face as if it were a loaded gun barrel. "Hey, that thing could go off!"

The pointed finger is usually only meant to emphasize what is being said. We still don't like it. It feels judgmental.

Daniel prayed, pointing fingers (he was confessing not only his own sin but also the sin of his people Israel). That seems easy to do. We love to point out other people's problems, and we are happy to do it in the privacy of our prayers to God.

While it may feel good to do that, Daniel began by pointing out his own sin first. He focused first on the three fingers pointed at him. Once he was cleansed and forgiven, he could ask for the cleansing and forgiveness of others. Remember, Daniel was confessing the people's sin to God, not confronting them about their sin. He wanted to step in for his people who refused to step up and repair their relationship with God.

Daniel wasn't actually pointing out their sin, he was confessing it and asking for their forgiveness. The focus was on forgiveness, not faultfinding.

DANIEL 9:23

"As soon as you began to pray, a word went out, which I have come to tell you, for you are highly esteemed. Therefore, consider the word and understand the vision."

D aniel prayed and met a high-ranking angel, Gabriel, face-to-face.

Think about it. We pray, and a dispatch comes over the loudspeaker at Angel Station.

"We have 625 in progress. Units needed to provide comfort." (625 is code for Matthew 6:25 about worry.)

Or "All units in the area, we have a call for a 613. Code red." (Matthew 6:13 says, "Lead us not into temptation.")

Gabriel said to Daniel "As soon as you began to pray . . ." Just like calling 9-1-1, without all the traffic in the way, angels rush to the call, designated by God to provide on-the-scene guidance, comfort to the victims, and protection from evil.

So think about your prayers receiving attention *as soon as* you pray. God and His angels are not encumbered by time, distance, or resources. They are on their way to help.

JONAH 2:1

From inside the fish Jonah prayed to the LORD his God.

You may never find yourself in the belly of a fish for three days, but if you did, and decided to pray, God would hear you.

This verse pretty much proves that you can pray just about anywhere and God will hear your cry.

Now, a fish belly would be a horrible place to be, disgusting and squishy, full of digestive juices and rumblings. It would be like smelly water torture. Imagine that for three whole days. It would be like lying in your grave, waiting to die.

You may wonder: *If God heard Jonah's prayer, why did it take three days to answer?* God was working on Jonah's heart. Jonah went from being a rebellious prophet to a humble prophet. God answered Jonah's need by providing comfort during that time. In chapter 2, he expressed hope to see the temple again, and he knew God would bring him up out of the pit. Maybe, logistically, the fish needed to travel from the deep sea to dry land. That probably took a little time. To answer Jonah's prayer by having him vomited into the middle of the sea would have led to Jonah's drowning.

So God hears your prayer from the depths of your despair, even while you wrestle in the belly of hell itself. It may stink, but God is working on the situation, giving you strength and hope while He orchestrates your way to safety.

49

MATTHEW 5:44

"But I tell you, love your enemies and pray for those who persecute you."

Pray for our enemies? Seriously?

We want to see our enemies suffer, don't we? We want them to realize that picking on us was a big mistake. Groveling? You bet. Apologies? Yes. We want to be right, and we want our enemies to feel sorry for being wrong.

Sometimes we use the expression "I would never wish that on my worst enemy." That's a nice sentiment, but we do wish some pretty bad things on our enemies.

So when we pray for our enemies, is it really for our enemies' sake that God wants us to pray for them? Maybe. But in the process, our attitude changes toward our enemies. When we begin to see them from God's perspective and not ours, our hearts may even break for them. We see them as not only hurting us, but hurting their relationship with God. We are reminded of our own sins and how we fall short of perfection.

Praying for our enemies levels the playing field, and we see them as more like us than against us.

MATTHEW 6:5

And whenever you pray, do not be like the hypocrites; for they love to stand and pray in the synagogues and at the street corners, so that they may be seen by others. Truly I tell you, they have received their reward. (NRSV)

According to Jesus, a hypocritical prayer wants some kind of a reward. The purpose of public prayer is to draw all people within earshot closer to God, not draw them closer to the person praying.

It's not "Look at me!" It should be "Look at God!"

Public prayer is all about motivation. Prophets in the Old Testament warned people through their prayers and called on God for protection. New Testament prayers drew people to Jesus and called on the Holy Spirit. All of them sought God's power.

Jesus said those who pray selfishly or to draw attention to themselves have already received their reward in full. What is that reward?

Maybe a few "Ooh's" and "Aah's" or pats on the back; someone saying, "That was a great prayer." That doesn't go a long way, but it may feel good for a little while, puffing up the pray-er. However, he receives no reward from God because he didn't do it for His glory.

Do you seek congratulations from people or communion with God when you pray in public? Ask yourself that before you start.

51

MATTHEW 6:6

"But you, when you pray, go into your [closet], and when you have shut your door, pray to your Father who is in the secret place; and your Father who sees in secret will reward you openly." (NKJV)

We use closets as storage places. Maybe we spend a minute or so in our closet getting ready in the morning (if it's a walk-in). Two minutes when you can't decide what to wear. When we look at buying a new home, closet space is very important, but once all our stuff is stuffed inside, we spend very little time there, popping in and popping out. However, according to Jesus, the greatest rewards are found in the closet.

Jesus' answer to the public-attention-drawing prayers He attacked in Matthew 6:5 was this: Go to your closet.

Long-sleeved shirts don't pat you on the back for such a passionate prayer. Pairs of gloves don't applaud your choice of words. Moths and spiders pretty much make up your audience in a closet.

Well . . . and God. God is happy to meet you in such a private place, void of any attraction or distraction. It's there He knows you only want His attention and His presence.

When your closet space becomes God's space, it will become the most important room in your house.

MATTHEW 6:7

"And when you pray, do not keep on babbling like pagans, for they think they will be heard because of their many words."

I don't know anyone who enjoys talking to a person who goes on and on about herself or himself and their activities. So many words to describe so little. "I went to the store . . ." becomes a ten-minute thesis on the parking situation, what clothes she wore, the weather, the crowds, the clerk who gave the wrong change (and what she was wearing). All that to say, ". . . and I picked up something for dinner." We might call that person vain because she loves to hear herself (or himself) talk.

This is how some people pray. On and on, with no real direction, or repeating themselves as if God didn't hear them the first time. It's unnatural.

We don't say to a loved one, "I love you, I love you, I love you" multiple times at once. It loses its meaning. One "I love you" said with sincerity and passion is all you need.

God doesn't want to hear babbling when we pray. We don't need many words or repetition. He wants to hear our heart, and He needs a little time to get a word in edgewise. Prayer is a two-way street, and God can't talk to you if you're driving the whole conversation.

MATTHEW 6:9

"Pray, then, in this way: 'Our Father who is in heaven, hallowed be Your name.'" (NASB)

Jesus taught His disciples to pray in answer to their request, so He gave them a model prayer (the next four verses cover that prayer).

This was not meant to be a magical incantation like *abracadabra* or *hocus-pocus* said over a situation. Nor is it a cookie-cutter prayer or a follow-these-instructions kind of prayer. Jesus did not intend for this prayer to be said blindly or mechanically without heart or thought.

Rather, His model prayer gave the disciples a guideline of what to pray for and how to pray. For example, the opening line identifies God in His holy place, to whom we should pray.

Our prayers should begin by recognizing our relationship with God. We pray to our Father in heaven, not to an automated answering service or a subordinate of God. If we call Him our Father, then we are His children. There's comfort in those words, security, and protection.

It's a familiar term meant to inspire heartfelt connection with a dad in heaven, looking down and watching over us. This father has the best view of our lives and He sees everything.

MATTHEW 6:10

" 'Your kingdom come.
Your will be done,
On earth as it is in heaven.' " (NASB)

In Jesus' model prayer, we acknowledge God's authority. His kingdom is expanded, not by land acquisition, but by heart acquisition. As more and more people come to fall in love with God, His kingdom expands. His kingdom has no borders; the loyal subjects of this kingdom live in many countries. Some are His followers openly, some secretly.

The kingdom operates according to the will of the king, whose decisions affect heaven and earth.

The will and desires of the king are carried out. Angels are busy, while the Holy Spirit gently guides.

His will affects the lives of those on earth. Some embrace it willingly, others defy Him. No matter the response, God's will is sovereign, and the final judgment is His.

We should pray that God's kingdom come to this earth, one heart at a time.

MATTHEW 6:11

" 'Give us this day our daily bread.' " (NASB)

Our daily prayers should be about daily bread. Not tomorrow's bread (you can pray about that tomorrow). Not dwelling on yesterday's bread (unless you forgot to thank God for it).

Focus on today's bread and God's provision. You may not get anything more than bread today, or a can of peas, or half a sandwich. Either way, you must be thankful.

If you got three full meals and snacks in between, you ate more than some people living in impoverished countries eat in a whole month. Don't feel guilty. Just give thanks.

We pray before meals to show our appreciation for our daily bread. We must never take it for granted. When we don't get our daily bread, we tend to complain and blame.

Receive your daily bread with a grateful heart, no matter what the quantity or quality. God has provided for you today.

MATTHEW 6:12

" 'And forgive us our debts, as we also have forgiven our debtors.' " (NASB)

Another important part of our daily prayer is to pray for forgiveness and to be forgiving.

This aspect of the prayer acknowledges that you will not only sin today, but someone will sin against you.

As surely as the sun rises and sets, you can be sure this will happen every day.

We don't start our day expecting to sin (though we're pretty confident someone will wrong us). Sin always sneaks up and surprises us. We don't schedule hate into our day or plan to lust right after lunch. In fact, surprise is all a part of sin's deception.

Eve wasn't prepared for temptation. Neither was David, standing on the rooftop of his palace (unless he knew Bathsheba's bathing ritual). Sin takes us off guard, knocking us off balance.

By praying for forgiveness, we are expecting sin in our day, taking away the element of surprise. When temptation strikes, we can respond by saying, "Oh yes, I've been expecting you." If we cave in to the temptation, we know what to do—restate that request for forgiveness that you've already prayed and also forgive others for getting you into that situation.

MATTHEW 6:13

" 'And lead us not into temptation, but deliver us from the evil one.' "

Is this verse saying God leads us into temptation?

God does not tempt us to sin. That's the devil's job. But God has power over Satan, who does lead us into temptation. The prayer asks God to stop Satan.

God does test us, our faith, and our resolve. That's what tests are for. To challenge us. To prepare us. Certain situations will come about that force us to rely on God more. We don't want to fail those tests by turning to the world for help. The tests can turn into sin if we try to cheat on the test or find shortcuts to good grades.

So this part of our daily prayer acknowledges that temptations will be a part of our day. The Evil One will be out to get us.

It asks God not to scrap all the tests we may face, but to help keep us from falling into the trap of temptation those tests may produce. We must call on the Holy Spirit to speak loudly and clearly so we will always find the way out of a tight spot.

MATTHEW 19:13

> Then people brought little children to Jesus for him to place his hands on them and pray for them. But the disciples rebuked them.

Jesus prayed for children. He took the time during His busy ministry to bless children and call on His Father to guide and protect them. But the disciples rebuked those who brought the children to Him. Why?

Children had no place in a busy rabbi's life. The apostles felt Jesus needed to deal with adult matters. Children were too immature, too loud, and generally misbehaved. They may have felt children were unclean, too, not observant of Jewish hygienic laws, many of them playing in the streets and touching who knows what. Possibly most of these disciples were single with no parenting experience and little patience.

Jesus spoke up and said, "Let the little children come to me, and do not hinder them, for the kingdom of heaven belongs to such as these" (v. 14). We must pray for our children, not just quietly in our rooms, but in their presence, placing our hands on them in blessing.

These are spiritual moments they will remember for the rest of their lives.

MATTHEW 21:13

"It is written," he said to them, " 'My house will be called a house of prayer,' but you are making it 'a den of robbers.' "

What is your church to you? A place to hang out with friends? A place of learning, with excellent teaching? A concert hall, with great music?

How about a house of prayer with God?

Jesus, upset by the trends of selling animals for sacrifice at the temple (sometimes at elevated prices) and currency exchange with travelers from other countries (sometimes at exorbitant rates), saw that the temple was becoming something other than what it was dedicated to be. It was to be the place where people met God, where God himself dwelt by His Spirit. While He is everywhere, and especially in the hearts of His people, the temple was the one location where He was sure to be found— behind the curtain (His presence in the Holy of Holies).

And just like your home is at your address, the temple was God's address on earth. Everyone was regularly invited to God's house to worship and offer sacrifices and prayers during the many festivals, such as the Passover. But it had turned into somewhat of a mad mall scene.

Today, the church is a place where you meet friends for fellowship, hear God's Word, and worship in song and in prayer. It is meant to be frequented every week, not just at special festivals like Easter and Christmas. Don't rob yourself, and God, of the invitation to worship at His house.

MATTHEW 21:22

"If you believe, you will receive whatever you ask for in prayer."

W ow! Of all the verses in this book, we could camp on this one the longest. It seems like the key to unlocking everything we want with prayer.

How can this happen?

Jesus had just talked to His disciples about cursing fig trees that didn't bear fruit and casting mountains into the sea. He said that if someone had faith and did not doubt, they could do those things. How can I get to that level of faith? Is it a matter of self-confidence, more trust in myself? No way.

Standing in front of a fig tree or a mountain with all eyes on me (and maybe some cameras for television coverage), I *would* doubt, especially fearing how ridiculous I must look.

The only way to vanquish doubt is to fully trust. I must know God's mind in a matter (this comes from a relationship with Him). I must be convinced that God wants a tree dead or a mountain gone. And I must not want to receive recognition or attention; it is God who must receive the glory for answered prayer.

So when we pray, we must first pray that God's will be done. He waits to hear our prayer, our prayer of faith. Believe that He wants to bless you. He *will* move mountains that stand in the way of His best for you.

61

MATTHEW 26:39

He went a little farther and fell on His face, and prayed, saying, "O My Father, if it is possible, let this cup pass from Me; nevertheless, not as I will, but as You will." (NKJV)

In Jesus' prayer to His Father at Gethsemane, hours before His brutal death on the cross, He asked that, if possible, "this cup" be taken from Him. The cup represented the wrath of God that would be poured out on Jesus as He took God's hatred of sin on himself on our behalf. We should bear the wrath of God and die for our sins, but Jesus took it upon himself so that we could go free.

Many think Jesus prayed this prayer because He was afraid of what was to come, that He was perhaps changing His mind about going through with it. Because He was a man, He would have some anxiety. The thought of enduring such pain would be hard to bear, at the least. But though His human side recoiled at the thought of the whip, the club, and the nails, He still prayed that His Father's will be done, not His own.

He wanted His Father's blessing and presence as He faced the guards, who would arrest Him in minutes. This was a prayer of confidence, not cowardice.

When we face trials and difficulties, we should pray for confidence and God's presence, and His will above all.

We want God to take away all the difficult times, but some of them need to be there. We can't run away when lives are at stake. We boldly must press on.

MARK 9:29

So He said to them, "This kind can come out by nothing but prayer and fasting." (NKJV)

As a child, when you got a stain on your shirt, your mom would say, "That kind of stain can only come out by soaking." Certain stains require specific attention.

Certain problems in life can only be corrected by prayer. In this account, Jesus had just healed a young man who had been tormented since childhood, being thrown down by a "mute spirit," sometimes in the fire, sometimes in the water, foaming at the mouth, and gnashing his teeth. The disciples tried to cast out the spirit but failed. When the father of the young man approached Jesus with his request, He was able to cast out the spirit. Privately, the disciples asked Jesus why they could not cast it out. Jesus told them this kind of problem required prayer and fasting.

No matter how much counseling the family might have received, or how much medication the doctors prescribed, or how faithful the family was in attending the synagogue or the temple—none of these things would have made the boy well. Only prayer and fasting.

It is hard to say which areas of our life or what illness or situation can only be resolved through prayer and/or fasting. We must use all the resources God has given us, and support them all with a persistent, focused prayer life.

63

MARK 11:24

"Therefore I tell you, whatever you ask for in prayer, believe that you have received it, and it will be yours."

Some people believe their prayers aren't answered because they don't believe enough. They blame themselves and carry around the guilt of not praying enough or not having enough faith when things go wrong.

Prayer isn't meant to produce guilt. It's meant to produce faith. Our prayers may or may not be directly related to the outcome. You can pray for world peace with all your heart, but it won't fully happen until Jesus returns. You can pray that your prodigal son returns to God, but if your son refuses, does that mean you didn't believe enough?

We must remember three things when we pray:

1. *Time*—our prayers will not be answered on our time schedule, but on God's.
2. *Free will*—our prayers are always up against the free will of the people being prayed for.
3. *God's will*—our prayers must coincide with God's will.

We cannot pray while blind to all these factors.

The best thing to ask for in prayer is that God's will be done. And we'll never be disappointed in His will.

MARK 11:25

"And when you stand praying, if you hold anything against anyone, forgive them, so that your Father in heaven may forgive you your sins."

An essential part of praying is forgiving. A lack of forgiveness can be a hindrance to our prayer.

Prayer is all about relationship. We communicate with our Father because we have a relationship with Him through Jesus Christ. In order for that relationship to be close, we have to be in close relationship with others as well. Remember the commandment given throughout Scripture: "Love your neighbor as yourself." You can't love God without loving others.

So if we're praying to God, but are in conflict with someone, our communication with God is interrupted.

We must forgive others because we are forgiven. God forgave us so we can be in relationship with Him. In the same way, we forgive others to be in relationship with them.

If you pray while forgiving others, your prayer life will grow deeper, and you'll remember that you are forgiven as well.

MARK 14:38

"Watch and pray, lest you enter into temptation. The spirit indeed is willing, but the flesh is weak." (NKJV)

Imagine what the spirit could do without the flesh. The flesh seeks its own satisfaction and comfort, from food to entertainment to relaxation. The flesh thrives on emotions and thrills, from love to roller coasters. The flesh wants to feel and see and taste, using all the senses.

The spirit of a person who is in fellowship with God seeks to please Him and do His will. The spirit desires the peace that comes only from God. The spirit unites with God's Spirit in worship, feeling God's presence and power. The spirit's faith and trust is in God's plan, and is at rest.

The flesh, on its own, wants what it wants. The spirit in tune with God wants what God wants. The two forces are diametrically opposed.

In the context of this verse, Jesus spoke to His disciples as they waited with Him in the garden and fell asleep while He prayed before His betrayal.

To us today, He would say, "Pay attention to your habits and your life so that you don't fall into the temptation of satisfying your flesh." Your flesh is very real, but it is weak. Your spirit, when in communion with God, is strong. Follow the leading of God's Spirit and grow stronger.

LUKE 5:16

But Jesus often withdrew to lonely places and prayed.

How would you describe a lonely place? A place where there's nobody around to bother you? A place where you might feel alone and wish you weren't? Or a place where there is no one to rely on for your spiritual needs except God himself?

Jesus found lonely places, away from the crowds that pressed in on Him for healing or teaching, or simply to question Him or to taunt Him. He went to places where there were no interruptions, no other support, except what He drew from God.

Jesus wanted others to know where He received His strength. We tend to turn to outside sources to tell us how to think and live, instead of going directly to the Source of all knowledge and guidance.

Some people think Jesus sought out the wisdom of gurus and shamans to grow in spiritual knowledge. The first time Scripture records Jesus talking to religious leaders was at the age of twelve. After that He generally attacked them for being fools or hypocrites.

The lonely place Jesus went to was a place void of books, speakers, and teachers because He sought the wisdom and voice of God alone to teach Him and guide Him.

And can any place really be lonely if God is there?

LUKE 6:12

Now during those days he went out to the mountain to
pray; and he spent the night in prayer to God. (NRSV)

College students know about all-nighters—late nights
spent studying and pulling in as much information as
they can at the last minute. The test the next day is very
important and worth more than a good night's sleep.

Jesus pulled all-nighters praying. Doesn't God want us to get
a good night's sleep? Don't our bodies need at least eight hours
of rest? Yes, but at times, what's more important?

If you spend a night in prayer because you feel it is needed
to intercede for someone or to seek God for special guidance,
you are saying that your relationship with God has top priority.
The time you spend with Him is more important than your time
spent any other way. Will it ruin your next day? Maybe. Will
your body be out of sync? Possibly. But what could be better
than spending eight hours in the presence of God seeking His
will and His presence?

We will always face tests and trials in life and, unlike the
college exams, these are not always scheduled. We have to be
ready at a moment's notice to face the pop quizzes of life.

LUKE 9:29

As he was praying, the appearance of his face changed, and his clothes became as bright as a flash of lightning.

Can you imagine praying and having your appearance change in the process?

Jesus prayed on the Mount of Transfiguration, and as He did, His appearance changed to reveal His true glory and identity as a person of the Godhead. The mild-mannered carpenter from Nazareth was truly the Son of God. The glow on His face and His clothing must have stunned those who were with Him—Peter, James, and John.

Though our appearance will not change when we pray, others in contact with us afterward may sense that we have been with Jesus. When His Spirit fills our lives, we will be changed people. You may be a mild-mannered accountant from Akron or a busy housewife in Boise or a small-town pastor from Poughkeepsie, but when you pray, you are part of that network of power generated by God's Spirit.

People will know you've been in the presence of God.

LUKE 11:1

He was praying in a certain place, and after he had finished, one of his disciples said to him, "Lord, teach us to pray, as John taught his disciples." (NRSV)

If you asked God to teach you one thing, would prayer be the first? Top five?

Personally, I would want to know how to better call to mind God's Word or the secret to quicker Scripture memorization, or how to lead someone to Christ or how to know God's will.

Apparently teaching about prayer was the hot topic in Jesus' day. John the Baptist taught his people to pray, and Jesus' disciples turned to Him for similar instruction.

There is more to prayer than quietly folding your hands in a closet every morning and repeating something by rote. And it's not the posture of prayer that is so important, but its purpose, its direction, its content.

What about knowledge, healing, evangelism? Aren't they important too? Come to think of it, if I prayed more often and with more purpose, maybe those other things would fall into place.

I want Jesus to teach me about prayer because it answers every other question of life.

LUKE 18:1

Then Jesus told his disciples a parable to show them that
they should always pray and not give up.

The parable of the persistent widow. Or, as it should it
be called: the parable of the nagging request.

Jesus told the story of a woman who wanted justice
from a judge, so she kept hounding him to vote in her favor.
The judge couldn't care less what people thought, but he caved
in and voted favorably for this woman.

So what does this say about prayer? I should just keep harping
at God over and over like a nagging kid in the backseat, crying,
"Have you answered my prayer yet?" until God snaps and says,
"Fine, I'll do it! Just stop bothering me!"

Is that the point of this story?

No. Jesus said that if a judge who didn't fear God or care
what anyone thought of him would grant the persistent request
of a widow, why wouldn't God, who loves His people, not grant
their persistent requests?

God responds to persistence, not because it bothers Him,
but because He loves us and He sees how much this prayer
means to us.

LUKE 18:11

"The Pharisee stood by himself and prayed: 'God, I thank you that I am not like other people—robbers, evildoers, adulterers—or even like this tax collector.'"

Prayer should never be an exercise in comparing and contrasting—rating yourself on a scale of haves and have-nots.

You can't pray effectively if you judge your situation based on the situation of others. Neither can you weigh your sins based on the sins of others, or analyze your reactions based on that of others.

If anywhere in your prayer you say, "I'm not as bad as . . ." or "Why can't I be more like . . ." you are off base.

Prayer is a time between you and God. If you compare yourself to anyone, it should be Jesus Christ. As you look to Jesus, you can then judge, weigh, and analyze yourself and see how far you have fallen short. Jesus is your barometer and your yardstick.

You may sin less than someone else, or behave better or give more, but it's never enough when you gaze at Jesus' perfection.

You're not in a race against others to win.

We've all fallen short of the goal, but because of Jesus, we all win.

LUKE 22:32

"But I have prayed for you, Simon, that your faith may not fail. And when you have turned back, strengthen your brothers."

J esus is praying for us? Wow.

He knows our weaknesses and our trials . . . and He's praying for us to overcome them all.

He doesn't want us to fail. He's praying for our success.

He has a plan for us. Once we've conquered our situation and Jesus' prayer is answered, there are jobs to do and people to see. We are not being prayed for solely for our benefit but also for the benefit of others.

If you could choose one person whom you would want to be praying for you, wouldn't you choose Jesus?

But Jesus' prayer has one limitation—our free will. Jesus prayed for Simon's (Peter) faith. Simon determined his faith, whether he would fully trust in God or trust in himself.

So yes, it's cool that Jesus is praying for you, but are you listening and lining up your will with His?

73

LUKE 22:44

And being in anguish, he prayed more earnestly, and his
sweat was like drops of blood falling to the ground.

An anguished prayer. A prayer that knows death is
imminent.
The condition—hematidrosis—is stress-related,
caused by blood vessels bursting near the skin's surface and
oozing out with human sweat. Sweat and blood.

Have you ever prayed that earnestly? Have you ever sweat
blood? Don't stress yourself out unnecessarily, but do you pray
with vigor and intensity? Is there anything on your prayer list
that gets you worked up? Things like . . .

- world events
- broken relationships
- medical crises
- lost souls

We all have something vitally important to pray for. Pray
as though someone's life depended on it, or someone's soul.
Prayer is serious business. It can hurt.

LUKE 22:46

"Why are you sleeping?" he asked them. "Get up and pray so that you will not fall into temptation."

Many of us fall asleep while praying. Why is that?

Our minds wander, thinking useless thoughts that eventually bore us, and so we fall asleep. It's the whole purpose behind counting sheep in order to fall asleep. As the mind engages in a meaningless task, it stops thinking about important things and naturally shuts off.

However, if we felt that counting those sheep was a matter of life or death, and unless those sheep got counted the world could end—then we might stay awake.

If we enter our prayer time thinking, *Oh, what does it matter* or *Who's really listening?* or *Nothing will really change,* our mind will start to wander around the universe, and we will fall asleep.

But if we pray thinking, *This prayer could change everything* or *Today could be the day God answers this prayer* or *This is a matter of life or death,* our mind will wake up and sense the urgency.

Nobody falls asleep during a crisis. Urgency keeps us awake.

JOHN 17:20

"My prayer is not for them alone. I pray also for those who will believe in me through their message."

W e must always be praying for people to come to Christ. We must be praying for those who are leading people to Christ as well.

There is always someone in your life who does not yet believe. Unless you've effectively evangelized everyone on your block, in your family, at your school/work. Congratulations! Or, maybe all your friends are Christians, which means you need to interact with some non-Christians and start praying for them.

Our prayers for the salvation of others directs our attention to the Holy Spirit's working in someone's life, and opens our eyes to opportunities to share the truth and invite people to places where the truth is spoken. Our prayers also center on other Christians coming into a person's life and influencing them in some eternal way. We may plant a seed, but someone else comes along and waters it. Everyone has an important part in the process.

Evangelists spread the good news from the city streets of New York to the plains of Africa. All of them need prayer for strength, wisdom, and opportunity.

There's no other prayer more important than the prayer for salvation.

ACTS 1:24

And they prayed and said, "You, Lord, who know the hearts of all men, show which one of these two You have chosen." (NASB)

The apostles needed to fill a slot in their group of twelve, left vacant by the death of Judas Iscariot.

In today's corporate world, the human resources department would put out a help-wanted ad, take applications, pore over résumés, go through several lengthy interviews, and contact three references for each applicant before coming to a decision.

Instead, the apostles prayed. In Acts chapter 1, they used lots to decide (equal to drawing straws or rock-paper-scissors). All that changed in the next chapter, when the Holy Spirit invaded their spirits at Pentecost. Now instead of asking God to use an outside means (lots) to show them the answer, they had an inside means (their spirits) to know God's will.

Whatever the means used to arrive at that decision, it began with prayer. The apostles knew they had an important decision to make, and they didn't want to rely on personalities or opinions. Interviews and references were not their way. They put their faith in God to make the right decision.

What decisions are you facing? Where do you start to come to that decision? Rock-paper-scissors is not recommended.

ACTS 2:42

They were continually devoting themselves to the apostles'
teaching and to fellowship, to the breaking of bread and
to prayer. (NASB)

The early church had their priorities straight.

It was a simple, purpose-driven structure, including teaching, fellowship, communion, and prayer. They focused on the Word, relationships among the group, remembering what Christ did for them, and asking God for strength and direction.

It was a good balance of truth, community, worship, and engagement. If any one of those factors took priority over the others, the church would wobble off balance. All four needed equal attention. If a church is all about the Word, it forgets the people. If it's all about the people, it forgets to worship. If it's all about worship, it forgets to pray.

Prayer must be a part of the church as much as the other three components—no more important, no less important, but sadly forgotten in many churches today. Make sure your church is praying—not just for the offering or in the benediction or some routine prayer that everyone knows by rote but doesn't come from the heart.

Pray that God will use the church to reach the lost. Pray for the needs of the people. Pray for leaders. Pray for maturity, growth, and direction. Corporately, the church should gather for prayer or it can get off balance.

ACTS 4:31

And when they had prayed, the place where they had gathered together was shaken, and they were all filled with the Holy Spirit and began to speak the word of God with boldness. (NASB)

Has the ground ever shaken when you prayed?

The chief priests and elders had just released Peter and John from prison, and the apostles reported to their fellow believers all that God had done. They had seen amazing responses to the gospel message, and many signs and wonders through healings and fresh commitments. So they prayed, and the room shook.

When we pray in faith, believing God hears us and is at work, it shakes up the world. We recognize when God is moving. We are sensitive to what is happening around us. We see walls come down and lives changed.

Sometimes we feel like our prayers are merely light breezes in people's lives, barely noticeable, that not much is happening.

But that is not true. We must see our prayers as earth movers and ground shakers. Peter, John, and the others prayed for boldness. Boldness is power. It comes from the Holy Spirit. Boldness is strength. His strength. Boldness is not a light breeze. It rocks the world.

So don't pray mindless prayers. Pray bold, ground-moving prayers.

And hold on . . .

ACTS 7:59

And they stoned Stephen as he was calling on God and
saying, "Lord Jesus, receive my spirit." (NKJV)

I f you were being stoned, what would be your first reaction?
Run? Scream? Curse? Throw the stones back? Stephen
prayed.

Stephen had been accused of blasphemy and had just given a
powerful defense to the crowd. Unjustly accused, he had every
right to defend himself, but his first priority was to pray.

Stephen prayed with confidence. He even asked that his per-
secutors not be charged with their sin. He knew where he was
going. He knew whom he served. What he didn't know was
the effect his death would have on the crowd. Some saw his
confidence and believed, wanting that kind of relationship with
God and assurance of heaven. Many ran away from Jerusalem,
frightened of persecution, and, in the process, spread the gospel
as God turned their fear into freedom for others.

Stephen's prayer opened up the heavens, and he had a vision
of the Lord Jesus at the right hand of God. It also opened up
the opportunity for many to hear and believe.

Let people hear your prayer as you face severe trials, so they
can know the God you serve.

ACTS 10:4

Cornelius stared at him in fear. "What is it, Lord?" he asked. The angel answered, "Your prayers and gifts to the poor have come up as a memorial offering before God."

Cornelius was a God-fearing man. He was responding to a vision of an angel in this passage. I can't imagine an angel showing up during my prayer time, can you? I'd probably scream or something. (Angels probably get that a lot).

Angels are God's messengers. In this case, an angel directly conveyed a message from God to His servant.

The angel knew Cornelius. He had a reputation in heaven for his prayers and gifts to the poor. And now the angel told him to send men to Joppa to bring back Peter. Of course, Cornelius was quick to obey, and sent two servants and a soldier to carry out the assignment.

So ask yourself—do you have a reputation in heaven? Are the angels talking about you or giving you messages from God?

If you spend more time in prayer, heaven gets to know you better.

ACTS 12:5

So Peter was kept in prison, but the church was earnestly praying to God for him.

I t's good to know that your church is praying for you, but some don't want their prayer requests known, embarrassed by their situation, or if the request appears on a prayer list, they don't want their name attached.

Peter was in prison for a good reason. It's easy to confess openly to the church that you're being persecuted for your faith. That's like a heroic reason to ask for prayer.

Others go to prison for their own crimes or are stuck in situations that become like prisons. Yet when it comes time for prayer, they hide their request, calling it "unspoken."

We need to know there are others praying for us specifically, and why not the church? The church is a group of people saved by grace. We're all sinners. We've all messed up at some time or other. We should be more open with our brothers and sisters in Christ than any other group so we can be assured they are praying for us.

Notice the church prayed *earnestly* for Peter. The word *earnest* means "characterized by or proceeding from an intense and serious state of mind: not light or flippant." The people were fully committed and engaged in their prayer for their persecuted brother. That's the way it should be, but the church can't pray for you unless they know you have a need.

ACTS 13:3

Then, having fasted and prayed, and laid hands on them, they sent them away. (NKJV)

The Holy Spirit told the church to separate Barnabas and Saul for the work He had called them to do. A common ritual we see in the New Testament is the commissioning of those sent out from the church to serve in other areas, spreading the gospel and doing the work of a missionary.

They did so through prayer and the laying on of hands. The laying on of hands symbolizes a connection or bonding between the senders and those being sent. Often pastors or other church leaders will actually lay hands on those being sent out, while the congregation extends their hands to join in the prayer and commissioning.

Commissioning services continue today. Those prayers cover the safe travels of those going out and the anointing of the Holy Spirit to work through those being sent, enabling fruitful labor, patience, perseverance, wisdom, and health to survive weeks or years away from home.

If you know someone who is heading out to do God's work, you can lay hands on them and pray for them, commissioning them as they go to serve; then continue to pray for them, letting them know that you are behind them every step of the way.

ACTS 16:25

About midnight Paul and Silas were praying and singing hymns to God, and the other prisoners were listening to them.

You have no idea who is listening to your prayers.

Paul and Silas were in prison for preaching the gospel, and were doing what they always did—praying and singing hymns. It came naturally to them. However, their actions were being watched and heard by fellow prisoners.

Don't be embarrassed to pray in public. There are others who need to hear how you cope and to whom you go for help and guidance.

Praying aloud in a restaurant may terrify you. You have no idea who is watching and thinking maybe they should be praying too.

This is not the kind of public prayers Jesus talked about in Matthew that were all for show. These are the normal, sincere actions of your faith that may be overheard or seen by others.

Don't be afraid of what others might think. God could use your boldness to draw others closer to Him.

ROMANS 8:26

In the same way, the Spirit helps us in our weakness. We do not know what we ought to pray for, but the Spirit himself intercedes for us through wordless groans.

ordless groans. Have you ever hurt so deeply or been so moved that the only thing your voice produced was a deep, guttural moan?

The original Greek here indicates grief expressed through a mournful sigh. This is a desperate groan. No words can express what you are feeling; there is no plan of attack, just a gut reaction.

The Holy Spirit groans and intercedes for us in our weakness. When we are in so deep, feeling so helpless, the Holy Spirit steps in and prays for us.

Notice this verse doesn't say the Spirit blames us, or puts us down, or chastises us when we're weak. (We beat ourselves up enough.)

No, when we need help, the Spirit "intercedes for us through wordless groans." He works in us and through us to make us stronger and get us back up on our feet.

85

ROMANS 12:12

Be joyful in hope, patient in affliction, faithful in prayer.

Ah, to be joyful, hopeful, and patient. Imagine life with all three of those qualities. A smile on your face no matter what you're facing . . . no worries.

It's hard enough just to be hopeful or just to be patient. You can't be any of those things by sheer willpower.

You only become joyful, hopeful, and patient when you are faithful in prayer. The last part of this verse causes the other parts to come alive in your life.

If you are a faithful person of prayer, you are placing all your problems before the throne of God. If you are a faithful person of prayer, you know that God is working behind the scenes to take care of everything, and that everything happens for a reason. Prayer puts you at ease because you put everything into the hands of God.

This faithful exercise of prayer strengthens you in the other areas, building up your joy, hope, and patience.

Let us be faithful in prayer . . . then rejoice!

1 CORINTHIANS 7:5

> Do not deprive each other except perhaps by mutual consent and for a time, so that you may devote yourselves to prayer. Then come together again so that Satan will not tempt you because of your lack of self-control.

The deprivation referred to here is sexual relations with your spouse. Paul said *don't deprive* each other *except by mutual consent,* so as to mutually devote yourselves to prayer for some particular crisis.

Keeping up a regular daily prayer life is not in conflict or competition with natural sexual relations in marriage. But like fasting from food, fasting from sex puts aside a preoccupation in order to concentrate on a particular prayer focus. The pleasures of this world and our natural life cannot be compared to the pleasures of a prayer life with God.

Remember, again, Paul emphasized mutual consent—both spouses agreeing on a predetermined amount of time.

The advice to resume your intimate relationship after a time apart prevents Satan from tempting you to step outside your commitment to your spouse in this area.

As a couple, agree to temporarily put aside intimacy with each other in order to emphasize your intimacy with God.

EPHESIANS 6:18

And pray in the Spirit on all occasions with all kinds of prayers and requests. With this in mind, be alert and always keep on praying for all the Lord's people.

Paul wrote to the church at Ephesus, and while wrapping up his letter, told them to pray in the Spirit on all occasions. This means to pray in a Spirit-guided, Spirit-infused way that is not following a routine or tradition, but a spiritual freestyle so to speak. A Spirit-led prayer is in tune with the Holy Spirit and follows His prompting.

Then, Paul was saying, once you're in sync with the Spirit, pray about all the things that affect your life—the weather, your finances, the government, fellow believers, enemies, your job, your neighbors, forgiveness, humility, war, peace, revival, your children, the elderly, life, and death. Pray about whatever the Spirit guides you to pray about.

By doing so, you are following the Holy Spirit's lead to keep you alert to all that is happening in the body of Christ.

Pray in the Spirit. Pray on all occasions. Pray all kinds of prayers. Be alert. Pray for all God's people.

There is a lot to pray about. What are you waiting for?

PHILIPPIANS 1:4

In all my prayers for all of you, I always pray with joy.

Joyful prayers.

Let's face it, most prayer requests are for the downers in someone's life—a bad medical diagnosis, job loss, divorce, prodigal kids, a car break-in, depression, or a vindictive neighbor.

So what are joyful prayers? Paul chose to switch his mood to joy instead of sadness, focusing on the good instead of the bad. We can always put a positive spin on a medical diagnosis—"Thank you, God, for leading me to the right doctor with the proper knowledge of my condition . . ." Job loss—"What a great opportunity for me to find a new direction in life." Divorce—"Turn this pain into joy, and help us to find an amiable solution to our differences." We can alter the mood of our prayers instead of getting pulled down into depression over the severity of our situation or that of others.

Remember, too, that when Paul wrote his letter to the Philippians, he was in jail. He managed to find joy in a hapless place and prayed confidently for people facing real problems.

Pray with joy, no matter what's happening in your life.

8⟨9⟩

PHILIPPIANS 4:6

Do not be anxious about anything, but in every situation, by prayer and petition, with thanksgiving, present your requests to God.

This verse is one of the greatest prescriptions for anxiety. It works for every situation you are facing.

1. *Pray*—talk to God about your worry.
2. *Petition*—ask, make your requests known.
3. *Appreciation*—be grateful that He hears your prayer and is working.

Now that you have presented your request to God, know that it is in good hands. He will orchestrate the best possible outcome for all concerned.

Worrying about something or being anxious does nothing to help the situation. Trust in God. You just handed over the details of your problem to Him.

Know that He has heard you. He is working. Be thankful, whatever the outcome.

No need to worry. There's nothing else you can do once you've given it all to Him.

COLOSSIANS 4:3

[And] praying at the same time for us as well, that God will open up to us a door for the word, so that we may speak forth the mystery of Christ, for which I have also been imprisoned. (NASB)

Paul said we should pray for open doors. What's an open door? An opportunity to share the gospel, maybe even lead someone to Christ.

We can pray that events in people's lives move them to become open to the gospel, even desperate for it. Financial crises, medical setbacks, moral dilemmas, divorce, death of a loved one—many situations in life cause people to seek spiritual answers.

Pray that people become curious about what the Bible has to say and ask questions. Ask the Holy Spirit to put thoughts in their minds, such as: *Is this life all there is?* or *Is there really life after death?* or *Do I matter to God or to anyone?* Once these kinds of question arise, people search for answers.

Pray that you can prompt the right discussions by what you say and have the right answers when the questions come.

The message of Christ is a mystery to those who don't believe. Many false ideas and teachings are spread among unbelievers. We can lift the veil of confusion by offering true and reasonable answers about God's love, Christ's sacrifice, and the help God's Word provides.

1 THESSALONIANS 5:17

Pray continually.

D on't stop praying.
Never give up.
Don't take a vacation from prayer.
Don't allow excuses to creep in.
Never think that prayer is useless.
Don't ever believe that God doesn't care.
Don't pray less, pray more.
Pray all the time.
Pray now.

1 TIMOTHY 2:1

I urge, then, first of all, that petitions, prayers, intercession and thanksgiving be made for all people.

This verse mentions all kinds of prayers for all kinds of people. There isn't such a thing as just one all-purpose prayer.

Petitions are requests made for specific needs. We ask, expecting an answer from God, while bowing to the will of God. We sign petitions to our government representatives to change policies. By petitioning God, we hope to change outcomes by asking God to intervene.

Prayers represent conversation with God, somewhat like when we call family to find out what's going on. Prayers don't have to be formal with a specific agenda each time, but can simply be time spent with our Father.

Intercession is standing in the gap for someone who is unable to pray or is being attacked by the enemy. We act as a mediator, such as a meeting organizer who steps in to bring the concerns and needs of others to those in authority. We keep the meeting on agenda until the problems are solved and all parties are satisfied.

Thanksgiving expresses our gratitude and appreciation for all God has done and is doing in our lives. Prayer can't be all problem-centric. We shouldn't only go to God with all the things that are going wrong; we should also take the time to thank Him for all the things that are going right.

These elements should be incorporated into all our prayers, giving a proper balance to our meetings with God.

1 TIMOTHY 2:8

Therefore I want the men in every place to pray, lifting up
holy hands, without wrath and dissension. (NASB)

By lifting up holy hands when we pray, we are indicating
our surrender to a holy God.

A person surrenders in war by lifting his hands and
saying, "I will not retaliate, fight, or argue. I'm yours to do
with as you please."

Our prayer time should begin with an attitude of humility
and surrender, knowing we are approaching a holy God, whose
power is unequaled.

We are not praying to "take on" God. We take on the posture
of a surrendered servant in order to pray aright.

Whether or not you physically lift your hands when you pray
is not important.

Surrendering your spirit is vital.

HEBREWS 5:7

In the days of his flesh, Jesus offered up prayers and supplications, with loud cries and tears, to the one who was able to save him from death, and he was heard because of his reverent submission. (NRSV)

Jesus prayed with passion.

As a member of the Trinity, the Son communicates with His Father in heaven on a regular basis. This communication happens on a supernatural level that we cannot comprehend (kind of like an eternally open hotline).

When Jesus came to earth, He separated himself physically and contained himself in a limited vessel—a human body. Now, to continue the eternal habit of communication with His Father that Jesus naturally desired, He needed to take time to pray. Time is not a factor in heaven. On earth it is.

This was different from what Jesus was accustomed to. With time so limited on earth, Jesus prayed fervently and tearfully, beseeching and pleading, and most important, He prayed submissively. He took full advantage of the opportunity, and used every means possible to communicate with His Father, unloading all His heart, soul, mind, and strength into His time of prayer.

JAMES 5:14

Are any among you sick? They should call for the elders of the church and have them pray over them, anointing them with oil in the name of the Lord. (NRSV)

Elders of the church are men and women of faith. They have years of experience with the struggles and successes of the Christian life and have matured to a point of leadership.

James tells those who are sick to go to the elders for prayer and anointing with oil. Elders cannot replace doctors, but they can work with doctors, especially when medical professionals have reached the limits of their knowledge and understanding.

Elders pray in the presence of the sick person, perhaps lay hands on them and anoint them with oil in the name of the Lord.

The anointing of oil symbolically represents the Holy Spirit, and His presence pouring over the person who is ill. Anointing also typically represents a special separation of the person for a specific cause or duty. Kings were anointed to show God's choice and calling. Jesus was anointed to show the presence of the Holy Spirit in Him.

The sick person is anointed, separating them for God's purpose and glory, and to be filled with the Holy Spirit.

While elders cannot guarantee healing, they can call on God for His mercy and intervention, and invite the presence of the Holy Spirit into the person's life.

JAMES 5:15

The prayer of faith will save the sick, and the Lord will raise them up; and anyone who has committed sins will be forgiven. (NRSV)

This verse seems to affirm that a prayer offered in faith for the sick will assure their healing. Many have prayed for healing, even calling in the elders in obedience to the previous verse. Not everyone who prays for healing sees the person raised up.

We might ask what is lacking—sufficient faith? We must not neglect the second half of the verse that says if sins have been committed, they will be forgiven as a result of this prayer. Of primary importance is our relationship to God. And sin separates us from Him. Illness does not.

Many times a prayer of faith offered for the sick does result in the Lord's raising that person up to full health and strength, but another way the verse could be interpreted would be that the prayer of faith will result in the sick person being saved from their sins and God completing their healing by taking them to be with Him forever.

We need to pray with faith, believing God can heal the body and heal the relationship between the person and God. God's will is not to make every sick person healthy while on earth. That is His will for heaven, for people to be resurrected in a new body.

The most important prayer is to pray for a person's salvation.

JAMES 5:16

Therefore confess your sins to each other and pray for each other so that you may be healed. The prayer of a righteous person is powerful and effective.

Good hears the prayer of a righteous person. They get God's attention. Righteous people are those who have accepted Christ as their Savior and thus have the righteousness of God in them because of Jesus' substitutionary death for them. Righteous people have a right relationship with God. They are more connected and have better discernment as to what God's will is in a matter. They've spent time listening to Him.

This doesn't mean their prayers are more spiritual or they are so righteous that God has to do whatever they say. A righteous person understands the will of God because they know the character of God and live in accordance with His will. They are obedient.

When they pray, they are more transparent—they have nothing to hide. They regularly confess their sins. Prayer requests are common. They put it all out there. They have been healed by confession and prayer.

They live the right way and know the right things to pray for. Righteous people don't tell God what to do. They know what God is going to do because they listen to Him.

1 PETER 3:7

> Husbands, in the same way be considerate as you live with
> your wives, and treat them with respect as the weaker
> partner and as heirs with you of the gracious gift of life,
> so that nothing will hinder your prayers.

Husbands, if you want your prayers to be heard, love your wives. Wives everywhere are happy to hear this.

Peter commanded men to be considerate of their spouses, treating them with respect. He didn't call women weak-willed or lower in status—quite the opposite—but told men to treat their wives more delicately. If a man disrespectfully abuses his wife because he thinks he outranks her, that man has an issue with God.

God tells husbands to see their wives as a co-heirs with them, equal in value in God's eyes, and eligible for the same eternal rewards in heaven.

A man can't be right with God if he wrongly treats his spouse. God loves her, and if the husband mistreats her, the lines of communication break down between him and God.

99

1 PETER 4:7

The end of all things is near. Therefore be alert and of sober mind so that you may pray.

While this may seem like a pessimistic way to view the need for prayer, it is actually quite realistic. It doesn't mean to pray doomsday prayers ("We're all going to die, so what's the use?"), but to pray knowing that life is short. There is an expiration date.

Also, as things wind down here on earth, drawing us closer to Christ's return, the verse implies that evil will grow in its influence and power. We need to be aware that events and evil powers will try to pull us and others away from God.

We need to wake up and pay attention to everything that is going on around us, giving us particulars to pray for. We have to be involved in people's lives and world events to know how to intercede and plead with God for others.

Our prayers should mirror current events and what's going on around us. We cannot pray effectively if we are uninformed or disengaged. We have to know what's happening so we know what to ask for and also to rejoice when our prayers are answered.

Yes, the end is always drawing nearer, but that doesn't mean God has stopped working or that we should stop praying.

REVELATION 8:4

The smoke of the incense, together with the prayers of
God's people, went up before God from the angel's hand.

The last book of the Bible shows us that during the final
and most trying days, the prayers of God's people will
rise up before God.

Incense in the temple always represented prayer, wafting up
through the rafters, skyward, reaching the heavens. Our prayers
please God, triggering a positive reaction from Him, like a
pleasant scent, reaching Him in the spiritual realm, drawing
His attention to the situation.

When smoke rises, it has no direct destination. It dissipates
in all directions, spreading its aroma everywhere.

Our prayers have no direct physical destination as they enter
the spiritual realm, and yet the impact of prayer affects many
people in all walks of life and in every corner of the world. It
is the impact of God working in their lives as a result of intercessory prayer.

Whatever is going on in the world or going on in your life,
continue to send your prayers heavenward. Prayers have a pleasing aroma to God.

God is waiting to hear from you.

SCRIPTURE LIST

1. Genesis 24:45
2. Genesis 25:21
3. Exodus 8:28
4. Numbers 21:7
5. Deuteronomy 4:7
6. Judges 16:28
7. 1 Samuel 1:10
8. 1 Samuel 1:27
9. 1 Samuel 12:23
10. 2 Samuel 7:18
11. 2 Samuel 7:27
12. 2 Samuel 24:25
13. 1 Kings 8:30
14. 1 Kings 13:6
15. 1 Kings 19:4
16. 2 Kings 6:17
17. 1 Chronicles 5:20
18. 2 Chronicles 7:14
19. 2 Chronicles 30:27
20. 2 Chronicles 32:24
21. Ezra 9:6
22. Ezra 10:1
23. Nehemiah 1:4
24. Nehemiah 4:9
25. Job 42:8
26. Psalm 5:2
27. Psalm 35:13
28. Psalm 55:1
29. Psalm 66:20
30. Psalm 69:13
31. Psalm 86:1
32. Psalm 141:2
33. Psalm 143:1
34. Proverbs 15:8
35. Proverbs 28:9
36. Isaiah 1:15
37. Isaiah 38:2
38. Isaiah 44:17

39. Isaiah 64:9
40. Jeremiah 7:16
41. Jeremiah 29:7
42. Jeremiah 42:3
43. Lamentations 3:44
44. Daniel 6:7
45. Daniel 9:3
46. Daniel 9:20
47. Daniel 9:23
48. Jonah 2:1
49. Matthew 5:44
50. Matthew 6:5
51. Matthew 6:6
52. Matthew 6:7
53. Matthew 6:9
54. Matthew 6:10
55. Matthew 6:11
56. Matthew 6:12
57. Matthew 6:13
58. Matthew 19:13
59. Matthew 21:13
60. Matthew 21:22
61. Matthew 26:39
62. Mark 9:29
63. Mark 11:24
64. Mark 11:25
65. Mark 14:38
66. Luke 5:16
67. Luke 6:12
68. Luke 9:29
69. Luke 11:1
70. Luke 18:1
71. Luke 18:11
72. Luke 22:32
73. Luke 22:44
74. Luke 22:46
75. John 17:20
76. Acts 1:24
77. Acts 2:42
78. Acts 4:31
79. Acts 7:59
80. Acts 10:4
81. Acts 12:5
82. Acts 13:3
83. Acts 16:25
84. Romans 8:26
85. Romans 12:12
86. 1 Corinthians 7:5
87. Ephesians 6:18
88. Philippians 1:4
89. Philippians 4:6
90. Colossians 4:3
91. 1 Thessalonians 5:17
92. 1 Timothy 2:1
93. 1 Timothy 2:8
94. Hebrews 5:7
95. James 5:14
96. James 5:15
97. James 5:16
98. 1 Peter 3:7
99. 1 Peter 4:7
100. Revelation 8:4

Troy Schmidt is an author and television writer with credits at Disney, Nickelodeon, Tommy Nelson, and Lifeway. He has written for Max Lucado's HERMIE AND FRIENDS series and was the consulting producer for *The American Bible Challenge* with Jeff Foxworthy. His other book titles include *Saved, Release, 40 Days, Chapter by Chapter, In His Shoes: The Life of Jesus,* and many others. Troy has also written several children's books, including *Little Tree Found* and *Their Side of the Story*. He is also a campus pastor at First Baptist Church of Windermere, Florida. Troy and his wife have three grown sons and make their home in Florida.